Primary Sources
of
American Symbols™

The United States Capitol

Jennifer Silate

The Rosen Publishing Group's

PowerKids Press™
PRIMARY SOURCE

Published in 2006 by The Rosen Publishing Group, Inc.
29 East 21st Street, New York, NY 10010

Copyright © 2006 by The Rosen Publishing Group, Inc.

Editor: Eric Fein
Book Design: Michael DeLisio
Photo Researcher: Amy Feinberg

Photo credits: cover Eyewire: American Icons; p. 4 (left) © Atwater Kent Museum of Philadelphia/Courtesy of the Historical Society of Pennsylvania/ Bridgeman Art Library, (right) Library of Congress Geography and Map Division; p. 7 (left) Courtesy of the United State Patent and Trademark Office, Office of the Under Secretary and Director, (right) Library of Congress; pp. 8 (left), 12, 15 (right) Library of Congress Prints and Photographs Division, pp. 8 (right), 16 (left), 19, 20 (bottom) Architect of the Capitol; p. 11 (left) National Archives and Records Administration, Records of the U.S. House of Representatives, (right) The Maryland Historical Society, Baltimore, Maryland; p. 15 (left) National Archives and Records Administration; p. 16 (right) © Corbis; p. 20 (top) © Wally McNamee/Corbis.

First Edition

Library of Congress Cataloging-in-Publication Data

Silate, Jennifer.
   The United States Capitol / Jennifer Silate.— 1st ed.
   p. cm. — (Primary sources of American symbols)
   Summary: A brief history of the United States Capitol with an emphasis on its role as an American symbol.
   ISBN 1-4042-2694-X (lib. bdg.)
   1. United States Capitol (Washington, D.C.)—Juvenile literature. 2. Washington (D.C.)—Buildings, structures, etc.—Juvenile literature. [1. United States Capitol (Washington, D.C.)] I. Title. II. Series: Silate, Jennifer. Primary   sources of American symbols.

F204.C2S55 2006
975.3—dc22

                                 2003021589

Manufactured in the United States of America

Contents

As commander of the American army, George Washington helped colonists win their independence from England in the American Revolutionary War (1775-1783). He was also America's first president.

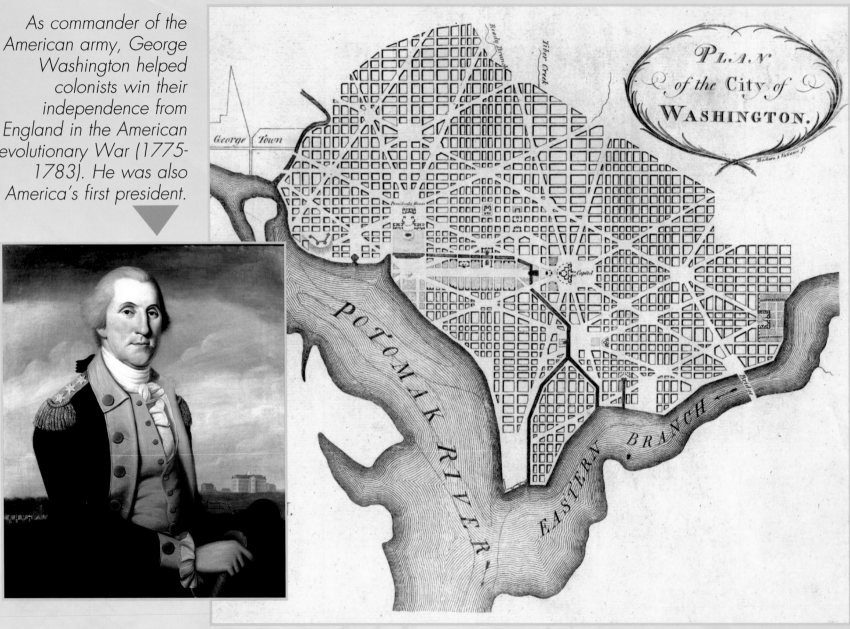

A Building for Congress

The United States Capitol is one of the most important buildings in America. For more than 200 years, the U.S. Congress has met there to write the laws that govern the country. Before the Capitol was built, Congress moved from city to city. However, by 1789, Virginia and Maryland had each offered 10 square miles (25.9 sq. km) of land to be used for the building of the nation's capital city.

In 1791, President George Washington chose the land offered by Maryland. The city was named Washington, District of Columbia (D.C.). Pierre Charles L'Enfant, a famous **engineer**, planned the **design** of the city. He was also chosen to design the Capitol. L'Enfant and Washington worked together to choose the spot where the Capitol would be built.

This 1792 drawing is Pierre Charles L'Enfant's plan for the city of Washington, D.C. Before the creation of Washington, D.C., the U.S. government had no official city and had met in eight different cities.

The Contest

In 1792, L'Enfant was asked to stop working on the Capitol because he had refused to give Congress a design for the building. A new designer had to be chosen. Thomas Jefferson, then **secretary of state**, came up with the idea of having a **contest** to find the best design. The winner would get $500 and a piece of city land. Seventeen designs were sent to the commissioners, the men that President Washington had placed in charge of the project. Unfortunately, the commissioners accepted none of the designs.

Months after the contest ended, William Thornton, a British-born doctor, sent a design for the Capitol. The commissioners and President Washington liked Thornton's plan. He won the contest.

William Thornton was a doctor in Scotland. He was also a self-taught architect, painter, and inventor. Thornton designed other buildings in Washington, D.C., including one that has become the home of the American Institute of Architects.

On March 14, 1792, an announcement for the Capitol design contest was placed in a newspaper. The announcement stated that the designs needed to include separate rooms for representatives and senators as well as meeting rooms and offices.

Ware, remarkably Cheap for

s to Rent, on Leafe, or Sell, which he lives, as may be Applicants

HAIR-POWDER, of the up for Exportation, or home Feb. 28. w&f

eaty, Silver-plater, LY acquaints his friends and general, that he has removed to No 147, Chefnut ftreet, and Fifth ftreets, where he E, with ftrong fheet silver, moft improved manner, every ch of bufinefs; and will ware equal to any imported from will furnifh complete fets of a cheaper rate than any other ; and has now for fale an ele- ir f horfes.   w&f2w

ed, and for Sale by
IN MASON,
of Market ftreet Wharf,
pply of Frefh
lover Seed,
l beft British
E TWINE;
n Affortment of
I L S.

pofing the whole mafs of the walls.
The Commiffioners.
March 14, 1792.

{ **WASHINGTON,** }
In the Territory of Columbia.

A PREMIUM,

OF a lot in this city, to be defignated by im- partial judges, and 500 dollars; or a medal of that value, at the option of the party, will be given by the Commiffioners of the Federal Buil- dings, to the perfon, who, before the 15th day of July, 1792, fhall produce to them, the moft approved plan, if adopted by them, for a Capi- tol to be erected in this City, and 250 dollars, or a medal, for the plan deemed next in merit to the one they fhall adopt. The building to be of brick, and to contain the following apart- ments, to wit :

A conference room ; Sufficient to ac-
A room for the Re- commodate 300
prefentatives ; perfons each.
A lobby, or antichamber to the latter ;
A Senate room of 1200 fquare feet area ;
An antichamber, or lobby to the laft ;

Thefe rooms to be of full elevation

12 rooms of 600 fquare feet area, each, for committee rooms and clerk's offices, to be of half the elevation of the former. Drawings will be expected of the ground plats, elevations of each front, and fections through the building in fuch directions as may be neceffary to explain the internal ftructure ; and an eftimate of the cubic feet of brick-work compofing the whole mafs of the walls.
The Commiffioners.
March 14, 1792.

Juft Publifhed,
BY THOMAS DOBSON,
Bookfeller, at the *Stone-Houfe,* in Second-ftreet, Philadelphia

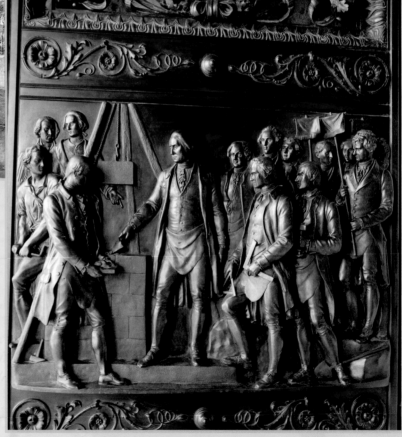

The north wing of the Capitol was the only part of the building finished by 1800. The north wing was shared by the House, the Senate, the Library of Congress, the Supreme Court, and other governmental agencies.

Building Begins

President Washington laid the **cornerstone** of the Capitol on September 18, 1793. Work had begun. Thornton did not have experience in building, so an **architect** had to be chosen to oversee the construction of the Capitol. James Hoban was chosen for this job. Hoban had earlier designed the White House. Work moved slowly. The **sandstone** that was used to build the Capitol had to be shipped from Virginia. The commissioners decided to work only on the north wing of the building at first. They wanted one wing to be completed before Congress was scheduled to be in the building in late 1800. Though some parts of the north wing were not finished in time, Congress was able to hold its first meeting in the Capitol in November 1800.

This plaster sculpture shows George Washington (center) at the laying of the Capitol's cornerstone. This sculpture is in the Senate wing of the Capitol.

Latrobe Gets to Work

Major work did not start again on the Capitol until 1803. Architect Benjamin Henry Latrobe was now in charge. Latrobe started work on the south wing. He added more offices and meeting spaces to the building. The **House of Representatives** was able to use parts of the south wing by 1807. The south wing was completely finished by 1811. Latrobe oversaw the rebuilding of the north wing too. It was already in need of repair. Latrobe also added a special meeting place for the **Supreme Court**. The Capitol would not be able to be finished yet, though. The year after the south wing was completed, the War of 1812 began. Latrobe left Washington, D.C. When he left, the north and south wings of the Capitol were still only connected by a wooden hallway.

This drawing shows Benjamin Henry Latrobe's floor plan for the part of the Capitol that would house the House of Representatives.

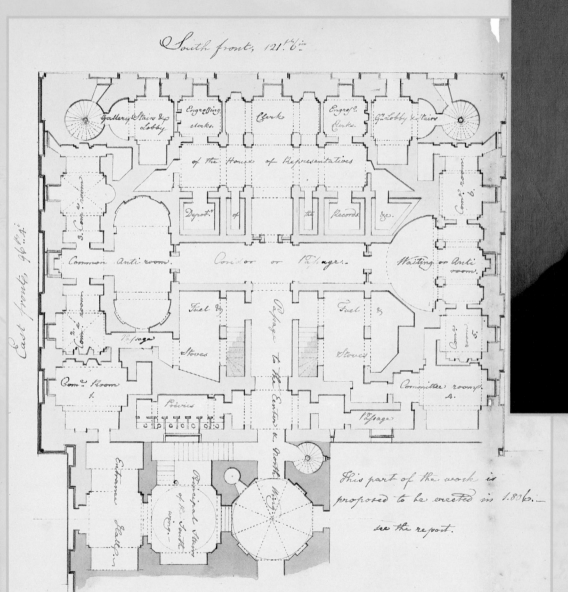

South front, 121 ft 6 in

Gallery Stairs & Lobby | Engrossing clerks. | Clerk | Engros? Clerks | Gall? Lobby & Stairs

of the House of Representatives

3 Com? room

Depot? of the Records &c.

Com? room 6.

Common Anti-room. | Corridor or Passage. | Waiting or Anti room.

2? Com? room

Fuel &c | Fuel &c

Passage

Passage to the Centre & North Wing

Stoves | Stoves

Com? room 5.

Com? Room 1.

Privies

Committee rooms 4.

Passage

Entrance Stairs

Principal Stairs of the South Wing.

This part of the work is proposed to be erected in 1806.—

see the report.

East front, 96 ft 4 in

▲

Benjamin Henry Latrobe was born and raised in England, where he became an architect. Latrobe came to America in 1795. He was the United States' first professional architect and engineer.

This picture shows Washington, D.C., being set afire by British troops during the War of 1812.

Burning and Rebuilding

During the War of 1812, British troops entered several U.S. cities. On August 24, 1814, the British took control of Washington, D.C. They burned many buildings, including the Capitol. Flames destroyed much of the inside of the building. Luckily, it rained the next morning. This rain soon put out the flames. After the war ended in 1815, the U.S. government started rebuilding the Capitol. Benjamin Latrobe returned to Washington, D.C., to start work again. This time, he chose to use marble instead of sandstone. Marble is a much stronger rock than sandstone. Latrobe worked on the Capitol until 1817. However, the work on the Capitol was still not finished.

◀ *The burning of the Capitol completely destroyed its middle section. The roof of the House of Representatives caved in and the room used by the Senate was destroyed. Over 3,000 books in the Library of Congress were burned.*

A New Contest

By 1827, $2,432,851 had been spent on construction of the Capitol. The building was more than 351 feet (106.9 m) long and 282 feet (85.9 m) wide. However, more space was needed for the growing number of lawmakers from the new states that were joining the Union. At this time, the Supreme Court and the **Library of Congress** also occupied the Capitol.

In 1850, the **Senate** held another contest for a plan to make the Capitol larger. The winner would get $500. However, Congress could not agree on one plan and it split the prize money between five architects. President Millard Fillmore chose Thomas Walter to be in charge of building the Capitol's **extensions**. On July 14, 1851, construction began on the Capitol once again.

Thomas Walter began practicing architecture in 1830. He was one of the founders of the American Institute of Architects. Walter was the architect of the Capitol until 1865.

This photograph of the Capitol was taken in 1846. It is believed to be one of the first photographs ever taken of the building. The Capitol is shown here with its original dome, which was made of brick, wood, and copper.

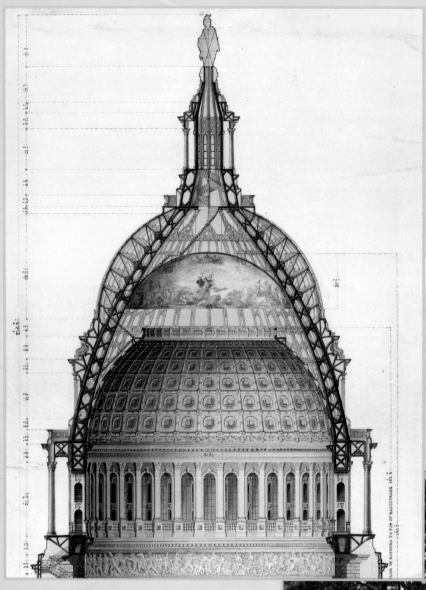

This is a detail from a larger drawing by Thomas Walter done in 1859. It shows his redesign of the Capitol's dome, including the addition of a sculpture on top of the dome. This sculpture would be designed by Thomas Crawford and be called the Statue of Freedom.

Construction Continues

Thomas Walter worked on the Capitol for 14 years. The addition of a new dome was his biggest change. In 1856, it was placed over the center section of the Capitol. The new dome was made of fireproof cast iron. It was 287 feet (89 m) high and weighed more than 8.9 million pounds (4,036,972 kg).

By 1857, the House of Representatives was able to use its **chambers**. The Senate was able to meet in its chambers by 1859. Work went well until 1861, when the **Civil War** began. For some time, the Capitol was used as a bakery, a hospital, and to house soldiers. In 1862, however, President Abraham Lincoln ordered work to continue on the Capitol. The Capitol's extensions were finally finished in 1868.

This 1864 photo of the Capitol was taken while the dome was still being built.

Art and History

There are many rooms in the Capitol. Some are no longer used for congressional work. The chamber once used by the House of Representatives became the National Statuary Hall. Each state was asked to provide a **statue** of two famous people from the state. These statues are in the hall and in other parts of the Capitol.

The old Supreme Court chamber is also no longer used by Congress. It has been remodeled to look as it did in the 1850s. Robes, desks, and figures of past Supreme Court justices are on display in the room. Many fine paintings and historical items are also kept in the Capitol.

The Capitol's National Statuary Hall has a collection of 97 statues that were given to the Capitol by the states of America. Forty-seven states have each given two statues. Three states have each given one statue and are allowed to give another.

This painting by Constantino Brumidi is on the inside of the dome, 180 feet (54.9 m) above the Capitol's Rotunda floor. George Washington is shown seated between two female figures. The other 13 figures standing in a semicircle around Washington represent the 13 original colonies.

This photograph shows the House of Representatives chamber during a presidential State of the Union address.

Keeping Up to Date

Construction to improve the Capitol has continued over the years. Indoor plumbing, electric lights, and elevators have been added to the building. These improvements were done in the 1880s through the early 1900s. Electric subways now connect the separate House of Representatives and Senate office buildings to the Capitol. The president has his own office in the Capitol. He uses it to sign the laws that Congress passes. The president also delivers the State of the Union speech from the House of Representatives chamber in the Capitol. This speech gives Congress and the American people important information about the country. The Capitol is a place where history has been made and continues to be made. It is a symbol of America's democratic form of government.

The U.S. Capitol is one of the centerpieces of Washington, D.C., and a symbol of the American way of life.

Timeline

1791	President George Washington chooses the 10 square miles (25.9 sq. km) of land offered by Maryland to be the capital city of the United States of America.
1792	A contest is held to select a design for the United States Capitol. Dr. William Thornton wins the contest.
1793	On September 18, President Washington lays the cornerstone of the Capitol.
1800	The north wing is used by Congress.
1803	Architect Benjamin Henry Latrobe begins work on the south wing.
1812–1815	The War of 1812 is fought between the United States and England.
1814	British troops burn the Capitol and other important buildings in Washington, D.C.
1850	A new contest seeking designs to make the Capitol larger is announced.
1851	Construction on the Capitol's extensions begins.
1861	The Capitol is used as a bakery, a hospital, and to house soldiers during the Civil War.
1862	President Abraham Lincoln orders work on the Capitol to begin again.
1868	The Capitol's extensions are completed.
1880s-1900s	Electric lighting, indoor plumbing, and elevators are installed in the Capitol.

Glossary

architect (AR-ki-tekt) Someone who designs buildings and checks that they are built properly.

chambers (CHAYM-buhrz) Large rooms.

Civil War (SIV-il WOR) The U.S. war between the Confederacy, or southern states, and the Union, or northern states, that lasted from 1861–1865.

contest (KON-test) A competition.

cornerstone (KOR-nuhr-stone) A stone forming part of a corner in a wall.

design (di-ZINE) To draw something that could be built or made; the shape or style of something.

engineer (en-juh-NIHR) Someone who is trained to design and build machines, buildings, bridges, roads, or other structures.

extensions (ek-STEN-shuhnz) Parts forming additions to a main structure.

House of Representatives (HOUSS UHV rep-ri-ZEN-tuh-tivz) One of the two houses of the U.S. Congress that makes laws. The number of members from each state is based on population.

Library of Congress (LYE-brer-ee UHV KONG-griss) A collection of books, records, and other materials held by the U.S. government.

sandstone (SAND-stohn) A kind of rock made up mostly of sandlike grains of quartz cemented together by lime or other materials.

secretary of state (SEK-ruh-ter-ee UHV STATE) The head of the U.S. Department of State.

Senate (SEN-it) One of the two houses of the U.S. Congress that makes laws. Each state has two senators.

statue (STACH-oo) A model of a person or an animal made from metal, stone, wood, or any solid material.

Supreme Court (suh-PREEM KORT) The highest and most powerful court in the United States. It has the power to overturn decisions made in lower courts and also to declare laws unconstitutional.

Index

Primary Sources

Cover: The United States Capitol. [Date Unknown]. **Page 4 (inset):** *George Washington* [c. Nineteenth Century]. Oil on canvas by Charles Peale Polk. Atwater Kent Museum of Philadelphia. **Page 4:** Plan of the City of Washington. [1792]. First printed edition of L'Enfant plan mounted on cloth backing. Library of Congress. **Page 7 (left):** *William Thornton.* [c.1804-1871]. Oil on canvas by Gilbert Stuart. U.S. Patent and Trademark Office. **Page 7:** Ad from *Dunlap's American Daily Advertiser* [March 24, 1792]. Clement's Library at the University of Michigan. **Page 8 (left):** *The North Wing of the Capitol in 1800.* [1800]. Artist Unknown. Architect of the Capitol. **Page 8:** *Cornerstone Ceremony Recreated* [c.1853-1857]. Plaster relief sculpture. Architect of the Capitol. **Page 11:** Floor plan of interior of the original House of Representatives [c.1806]. Benjamin Henry Latrobe. National Archives. **Page 11 (inset):** *Benjamin Henry Latrobe.* [c. 1815]. Oil on canvas by Rembrandt Peale. Maryland Historical Society. **Page 12 (inset):** The taking of the city of Washington in America. [c. 1814]. Print of wood engraving published by G. Thompson. Artist unknown. Library of Congress. **Page 12:** A view of the Capitol of the United States after the Conflagration of 24 August 1814. [1814]. George Munger. Library of Congress. **Page 15 (left):** Thomas Walter [c.1860-1865]. National Archives. **Page 15:** The Capitol's East Front in 1846. [1846]. Architect of the Capitol. **Page 16 (left):** Section Through Dome of U.S. Capitol. [1859]. Ink and watercolor on paper by Thomas U. Walter. Architect of the Capitol. **Page 16:** U.S. Capitol with Unfinished Dome [c.1864]. **Page 19 (left):** National Statuary Hall Viewed from the Southwest [2001]. Architect of the Capitol. **Page 19:** *The Apotheosis of Washington* [1865]. Fresco by Constantino Brumidi. Architect of the Capitol. **Page 20 (inset):** State of the Union Address [1997]. **Page 20:** Aerial View of the U.S. Capitol and Grounds from the West. [2001]. Architect of the Capitol.

Web Sites

Due to the changing nature of Internet links, PowerKids Press has developed an on-line list of Web sites related to the subject of this book. This site is updated regularly. Please use this link to access the list:
http://www.powerkidslinks.com/psas/usc/